THE FASCINATING
BUG
BOOK
FOR KIDS

THE FASCINATING
BUG
BOOK
FOR KIDS

500
STARTLING
FACTS!

KRYSTAL MONIQUE TONEY

ROCKRIDGE
PRESS

TO ELLA, ANNA, AND TRACEY,
WHO TOLERATED MY LOVE OF INSECTS AND
ALLOWED ME TO STORE THEM IN THE FREEZER.
"BUGGING" YOU ALL HAS BEEN
THE GREATEST ADVENTURE.

Rockridge Press publishes its books in a variety of electronic and print formats. Some content that appears in print may not be available in electronic books, and vice versa.

TRADEMARKS: Rockridge Press and the Rockridge Press logo are trademarks or registered trademarks of Callisto Media Inc. and/or its affiliates, in the United States and other countries, and may not be used without written permission. All other trademarks are the property of their respective owners. Rockridge Press is not associated with any product or vendor mentioned in this book.

Series Designer: Linda Snorina
Interior and Cover Designer: Jill Lee
Art Producer: Hannah Dickerson
Editor: Maxine Marshall
Production Editor: Ellina Litmanovich
Production Manager: Eric Pier-Hocking

Photography © Mark Bowler/Science Source, p. V; Erik Karits/iStock, p. 1; Richard Becker/Alamy Stock Photo, p. 95 (top left); blickwinkel/Alamy Stock Photo, p. 95 (top right); David Shale/NaturePL/Science Source, p. 132 (right);
Nature Picture Library/Alamy Stock Photo, p. 133 (right); Nuridsany et Perennou/Science Source, p. 157 (top left); Ted Kinsman/Science Source, p. 165 (left); Brian Enting/Science Source, p. 165 (right); John Cancalosi/Alamy Stock Photo, p. 183 (top left); Mira/Alamy Stock Photo, p. 189 (right);
Louise Murray/Alamy Stock Photo, p. 197 (top left); All other photography used under license from Shutterstock.com. Author photo courtesy of Victoria Nichole.

Paperback ISBN: 978-1-63878-065-6
eBook ISBN: 978-1-63807-668-1
R0

Chapter 1

DISCOVERING BUGS

BUGS ARE THE MOST DIVERSE AND ABUNDANT ANIMALS ON EARTH. THEY ARE FOUND EVERYWHERE, FROM THE FRIGID ICE FIELDS OF ANTARCTICA TO THE SWELTERING DESERTS OF AFRICA.

A HISTORY OF BUGS

INSECTS HAVE BEEN AROUND FOR MORE THAN 350 MILLION YEARS. THEY WERE HERE BEFORE THE DINOSAURS!

Over one million species of insects have been discovered. Researchers estimate that there could be as many as nine million species left to discover.

BUGS MAKE UP 90 PERCENT OF ALL KNOWN SPECIES OF ANIMALS ON PLANET EARTH.

All insects are bugs. But not all bugs are insects. "BUG" is a general word for all arthropods, or animals that lack backbones.

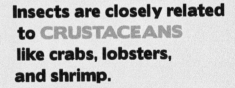

Insects are closely related to CRUSTACEANS like crabs, lobsters, and shrimp.

When food is available, bugs reproduce rapidly, which helps their populations stay so large.

ALL ABOUT ARTHROPODS

ARTHROPODS HAVE SEGMENTED BODIES.

Insects (like bees and ants), crustaceans (like crabs and lobsters), arachnids (like spiders and scorpions), and myriapods (like millipedes and centipedes) all belong to a group of animals called ARTHROPODS.

Arthropods have **EXOSKELETONS**, which are hard coverings that protect their bodies.

Arthropods make up the largest phylum in the animal kingdom. **"PHYLUM"** is a term used by scientists to classify different animals and things found in nature.

3, 4, 5 . . . 6 LEGS!

TWO-THIRDS OF ALL FLOWERING PLANTS ARE POLLINATED BY HEXAPODS.

There are over **ONE MILLION** species of hexapods, a type of arthropod that has six legs.

ALL INSECTS ARE HEXAPODS.

Hexapods are extremely **DIVERSE**. There are more species of hexapods than all the other animals in the world combined.

MOST HEXAPODS ARE TERRESTRIAL, WHICH MEANS THEY LIVE ON LAND, BUT SOME LIVE IN LAKES OR RIVERS.

INTERESTING INSECTS

INSECTS CAN "FART" BY RELEASING GAS PRODUCED BY DIGESTION THROUGH THEIR SPIRACLES, THE HOLES THROUGH WHICH THEY BREATHE.

An **ORDER** is a group of plants or animals with similar features (there are about 30 orders of insects). Beetles are in the order Coleoptera. Moths and butterflies are in the order Lepidoptera.

INSECTS EAT PLANTS, ANIMALS, BLOOD, AND EVEN OTHER INSECTS.

Insects are INVERTEBRATES, which means they do not have backbones.

CRUSTACEANS: BUGS OF THE SEA

THERE HAVE BEEN 50,000 TO 67,000 SPECIES OF CRUSTACEANS IDENTIFIED WORLDWIDE. THAT'S ALMOST TWICE THE NUMBER OF KNOWN SPECIES OF FISH IN THE SEA!

Wood lice and terrestrial hermit crabs are crustaceans that live on land.

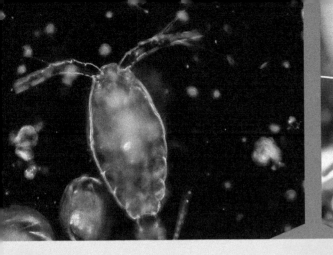

CRUSTACEANS CAN BE AS SMALL AS MICROSCOPIC PLANKTON OR AS LARGE AS A GIANT CRAB, WHICH CAN WEIGH UP TO 40 POUNDS (18 KG). THAT'S HEAVIER THAN AN AVERAGE THREE-YEAR-OLD CHILD!

Crustaceans like to live in environments with water, and they are most diverse within the world's oceans.

While many animals evolve to look different over time, the **MANTIS SHRIMP** has remained the same as it was during the Miocene age, between 5.3 and 23 million years ago.

5, 6, 7 . . . 8 LEGS!

ARACHNIDS HAVE MANY LEGS, BUT NO ANTENNAE OR WINGS.

BUGS WITH EIGHT LEGS ARE CALLED ARACHNIDS.

Arachnids have only two body segments: the **CEPHALOTHORAX** (a combination of head and thorax) and the **ABDOMEN**.

MOST ARACHNIDS ARE CARNIVOROUS (MEANING THEY EAT MEAT). THEY FEED ON INSECTS AND OTHER SMALLER ANIMALS.

SO FAR, 100,000 SPECIES OF ARACHNIDS HAVE BEEN DISCOVERED, BUT SCIENTISTS BELIEVE THERE COULD BE AS MANY AS 600,000 SPECIES ON EARTH.

Spiders aren't the only arachnids. Scorpions and mites are arachnids, too!

MANY-LEGGED MYRIAPODS

MILLIPEDE MEANS "1,000 FEET," BUT SOME MILLIPEDES HAVE ONLY 80 FEET.

BUGS WITH LOTS OF LEGS ARE CALLED MYRIAPODS.

Centipede means "100 FEET," but some centipedes have as many as 300 feet!

14

ABOUT
15,000 SPECIES
OF MYRIAPODS
ARE ALIVE TODAY.
THAT'S ALMOST
THREE TIMES
THE NUMBER OF
KNOWN SPECIES
OF MAMMALS
ALIVE TODAY!

The oldest myriapod fossil is
about 420 million years old.
That's more than
300 million years older than
a *Tyrannosaurus rex*!

Myriapods have two
body segments: the
head and the trunk.

TRUE OR FALSE . . . TRUE BUGS!

THE BUGS THAT WE CALL "TRUE BUGS" ARE IN THE ORDER HEMIPTERA, WHICH MEANS "HALF WING."

True bugs have piercing mouthparts. Their mouths look like long needles or straws, which they use to slurp up their food.

TRUE BUGS CAN BE FOUND IN ALMOST ANY HABITAT ON LAND AND IN WATER.

Land-living true bugs are herbivores and use their mouthparts to suck sap from plants.

THERE ARE ABOUT 85,000 SPECIES OF TRUE BUGS WORLDWIDE. ABOUT 11,000 SPECIES LIVE IN NORTH AMERICA.

CLOSE-UP ON CAMEL SPIDERS

CAMEL SPIDERS CAN GROW UP TO 6 INCHES (15 CM) LONG, ABOUT THE LENGTH OF A SALAD FORK.

CAMEL SPIDERS AREN'T ACTUALLY SPIDERS. THEY ARE ARACHNIDS, BUT THEY BELONG TO THE ORDER SOLIFUGAE, WHICH MEANS "THOSE WHO FLEE FROM THE SUN."

CAMEL SPIDERS LIVE IN THE DESERT AND ARE DIFFICULT TO FIND AND STUDY, MAKING THEM SOME OF THE MOST MYSTERIOUS ARACHNIDS IN THE WORLD!

The fastest camel spiders can run at about 10 miles per hour (16 kph). That's more than twice the average walking speed of humans.

Camel spiders eat anything they can catch and hold. Larger camel spiders eat lizards, snakes, mice, and even small birds.

HEY THERE, HONEYBEE!

EACH HONEYBEE COLONY HAS ONLY ONE QUEEN.

WORKER BEES are female, and their job is to gather food and protect the hive. The average worker bee lives for five to six weeks.

ALL DRONE HONEYBEES ARE MALE, AND THEIR JOB IS TO MATE WITH THE QUEEN.

If the queen honeybee dies, the worker bees will feed a young larva special food called ROYAL JELLY that will help it develop into a new queen.

Honeybees live in hives or colonies, where they are either workers or drones.

EVEN THOUGH THEIR BRAINS ARE ONLY THE SIZE OF A SESAME SEED, BEES HAVE EXCELLENT MEMORIES AND CAN EVEN DO SIMPLE MATH.

HORSESHOE CRABS

HORSESHOE CRABS ARE MORE CLOSELY RELATED TO SPIDERS AND TICKS THAN TO CRABS.

Horseshoe crabs have been on Earth for around 220 million years. They're older than dinosaurs!

HORSESHOE CRABS GOT THEIR NAME FROM THE SHAPE OF THEIR EXOSKELETON. DO YOU THINK THEY LOOK LIKE HORSESHOES?

HORSESHOE CRABS HAVE 10 EYES!

HORSESHOE CRABS ARE IN A CLASS OF THEIR OWN CALLED MEROSTOMATA. "CLASS" IS A TERM USED BY SCIENTISTS TO DESCRIBE A GROUP OF RELATED ANIMALS.

MAGNIFICENT MILLIPEDES

MILLIPEDES ARE SCAVENGERS AND HERBIVORES, MEANING THEY EAT PLANTS.

When threatened, millipedes release **SMELLY OOZE** from glands along their bodies to protect themselves from predators.

Each time a millipede MOLTS, or sheds its EXOSKELETON, it adds more body segments and legs.

WHEN A MILLIPEDE HATCHES, IT HAS ONLY THREE PAIRS OF LEGS.

Millipedes burrow into the soil to build nests in which they lay their eggs.

25

PILL BUGS

PILL BUGS ARE **CRUSTACEANS THAT LIVE ON LAND.**

Pill bugs are NOCTURNAL. They spend the day in dark, humid places like under fallen leaves or rocks.

PILL BUGS NEED TO LIVE IN WET, HUMID ENVIRONMENTS TO SURVIVE. THEY DON'T LIKE TO GET TOO HOT OR DRY!

Pill bugs are more closely related to shrimp and crayfish than to any kind of insect.

PILL BUGS SHED THEIR EXOSKELETON 12 OR MORE TIMES THROUGHOUT THEIR LIVES.

OLDER THAN DIRT: ANCIENT INSECTS

THERE ARE 30 ORDERS OF INSECTS KNOWN TO HAVE EXISTED DURING THE PERMIAN PERIOD. THIS PERIOD TOOK PLACE 250 TO 290 MILLION YEARS AGO WHEN ALL OF THE WORLD'S LANDMASSES WERE CONNECTED IN A SINGLE, GIANT CONTINENT.

SCIENTISTS BELIEVE THAT THE COCKROACH IS THE MOST ANCIENT WINGED INSECT.

The oldest known **INSECT FOSSIL** is the *Rhyniognatha hirsti*. Scientists believe the insect, less than an inch (2.5 cm) long, looked like a **CENTIPEDE** when it was alive.

SCIENTISTS THINK THE *RHYNIOGNATHA HIRSTI* FOSSIL IS ABOUT 400 MILLION YEARS OLD.

FOSSIL RECORDS OF SOME DRAGON-FLIES SHOW THAT THEY WERE GIANT INSECTS WITH WINGSPANS OF UP TO 28 INCHES (71 CM). THAT'S ALMOST AS LONG AS A BASEBALL BAT!

THE IMPACT OF INSECTS

THERE ARE MORE THAN 250,000 KINDS OF FLOWERING PLANTS. HONEY BEES VISIT AND POLLINATE 80 PERCENT OF THESE SPECIES. THOSE ARE SOME BUSY BEES!

SCALE INSECTS produce dyes that are used in medicine and beverages and to make food coloring.

Most of the silk that we use in clothing and bedsheets is produced from the cocoons of SILKWORMS.

IN SOME CULTURES AROUND THE WORLD, INSECTS ARE EATEN BECAUSE THEY ARE HIGH IN PROTEIN.

FRUIT FLIES are used in many scientific studies due to their short life span (about 10 days).

BUGS FOR BREAKFAST

THE VENUS FLYTRAP IS A CARNIVOROUS PLANT THAT EATS BUGS! IT LURES BUGS INTO A MOUTHLIKE CHAMBER, THEN QUICKLY CLOSES IT, TRAPPING THEM INSIDE.

OPOSSUMS ARE NATURE'S PEST CONTROLLERS. THEY LOVE TO EAT TICKS AND CAN EAT UP TO 4,000 OF THEM IN A WEEK.

A GIANT ANTEATER CAN EAT 35,000 ANTS AND TERMITES EVERY DAY.

INSECTS ARE AN IMPORTANT PART OF ANY ECOSYSTEM. THEY PROVIDE FOOD FOR BIRDS, REPTILES, FISH, MAMMALS, AMPHIBIANS, AND EVEN PLANTS!

The bird called the BLUE TIT feeds its chicks up to 10,000 caterpillars in just three to four weeks!

There are more than 900 species of bats in the world. Most of them prey on insects and can eat half their body weight in insects in a single night.

Chapter 2

BUGGY BODIES

BUGS ARE EXTREMELY ADAPTABLE. THEY HAVE UNIQUE BODY PARTS SO THEY CAN SEE, HEAR, SMELL, EAT, DRINK, AND JUMP IN MANY ENVIRONMENTS.

BUG ANATOMY

UNLIKE OUR STOMACHS, THE STOMACH OF AN INSECT IS A LONG TUBE WITH THREE SEPARATE PARTS: THE FOREGUT, THE MIDGUT, AND THE HINDGUT.

Bug blood is called HEMOLYMPH. It is not red like your blood! It is clear with a hint of green or yellow.

INSECTS ARE THE ONLY BUGS THAT HAVE WINGS—CRUSTACEANS, ARACHNIDS, AND OTHER CREEPY-CRAWLIES DO NOT HAVE WINGS. THERE ARE SOME INSECTS, THOUGH, LIKE LICE AND FLEAS, THAT DON'T HAVE WINGS.

Bugs have an OPEN CIRCULATORY SYSTEM, which means they don't have arteries or veins.

FLYING HIGH

A BEETLE HAS TWO PAIRS OF WINGS BUT USES ONLY ONE PAIR TO FLY. THE OTHER PAIR IS A HARD CASE, CALLED THE ELYTRA, THAT PROTECTS THE FLYING WINGS.

A LACEWING can move its front and hind wings independently to swiftly change direction midflight.

A BUTTERFLY'S FRONT WINGS AND HIND WINGS ARE HOOKED TOGETHER AND FLAP AT THE SAME TIME.

HAWK MOTHS are some of the fastest flying insects in the world. They can fly at 30 mph (48 kph). That's as fast as a car on most neighborhood streets!

The hind wings of flies have evolved into HALTERES that are used for steering. The halteres are little bars that help the fly keep its balance while flying.

THE HOVERFLY FLAPS ITS WINGS 1,000 TIMES PER SECOND!

EXOSKELETONS: ARMOR FOR BUGS

BECAUSE AN EXOSKELETON IS STIFF AND HARD, IT DOES NOT GROW WHEN THE BUG GROWS. INSTEAD, BUGS SHED, OR MOLT, THEIR OLD EXOSKELETON AND GROW A NEW ONE.

An insect's muscles attach directly to its exoskeleton—there's no skin in between!

THE EXOSKELETONS OF
CRABS, SCORPIONS, AND
OTHER ARTHROPODS
ARE MADE FROM A HARD,
WATERPROOF MATERIAL
CALLED CHITIN.

The exoskeleton is like armor
on the outside of a bug's body
that protects it from predators.

The IRONCLAD BEETLE'S exoskeleton is so
strong that it can survive being run over by a car.

HOW DO BUGS BREATHE?

TOO MUCH OXYGEN CAN HURT AN INSECT'S BODY. WHEN AN INSECT HAS ENOUGH OXYGEN, IT CAN HOLD ITS BREATH FOR DAYS!

Insects breathe through tiny holes along their bodies called **SPIRACLES**. Air comes in through the spiracles and into tubes called **TRACHEA**, which carry it to other parts of the insect's body.

ARACHNIDS BREATHE EITHER THROUGH BOOK LUNGS, THIN PLATES OF TISSUE LOCATED ON THEIR ABDOMENS, OR THROUGH A TRACHEAL SYSTEM SIMILAR TO SPIRACLES IN INSECTS.

INSECTS CAN OPEN AND CLOSE THEIR SPIRACLES BY CONTRACTING THEIR MUSCLES.

Scientists believe that spiracles evolved from the gills of ancient fish.

BUG-EYED

HONEYBEES HAVE TWO COMPOUND EYES AND THREE SIMPLE EYES.

Honeybees' eyes are hairy, so if they get dirty, they have to comb them.

44

Bees and ants have simple eyes, or OCELLI, that help them detect light and movement.

MANY INSECTS HAVE TWO EYES, BUT SOME INSECTS HAVE AS MANY AS FIVE.

Some bugs, like flies and beetles, have compound eyes, which are made up of hundreds (or even thousands!) of tiny "MIRRORS" known as FACETS that help bugs see.

45

MOUTHY MANDIBULATE INSECTS

MOST INSECTS HAVE MOUTHPARTS THAT CAN GRIND, CHEW, PINCH, OR CRUSH SOLID FOODS. THESE ARE CALLED MANDIBULATE MOUTHPARTS.

The mandibulate mouthparts of **HOUSEFLIES** and **BLOWFLIES** are specialized for sponging up liquid foods.

GROUND BEETLES are predators with mandibulate mouthparts that point forward to allow them to catch prey.

GRASSHOPPERS HAVE MANDIBULATE MOUTHPARTS THAT POINT DOWNWARD SO THEY CAN EASILY CHEW LEAVES.

The two most common mandibulate mouthparts found on insects are chewing mouths and piercing or sucking mouths.

NICE LEGS!

THE LEGS OF WATER STRIDERS CAN SUPPORT THEIR BODIES ON THE SURFACE OF WATER.

BEES' LEGS CAN CARRY SMALL AMOUNTS OF POLLEN.

A centipede's first two legs are modified fangs. This means that the legs evolved from fangs over time to perform a new job.

GRASSHOPPERS have legs adapted to be able to jump up to 30 inches (76 cm). That's like a human jumping from one side of a football field to the other in one leap!

LICE use their legs to grasp and cling to strands of hair.

ARTHROPODS USE THEIR LEGS FOR WALKING, BUT SOME ALSO HAVE SPECIAL LEGS FOR GRASPING, PROBING, OR SWIMMING.

STRONG AS HERCULES

ANTS CAN LIFT 50 TIMES THEIR BODY WEIGHT. THAT'S EQUIVALENT TO A HUMAN LIFTING AN ELEPHANT!

COCONUT CRABS are the largest terrestrial (or land-living) crustaceans and can lift almost 66 pounds (30 kg). That's more than a husky dog weighs!

A PRAYING MANTIS is a very strong predator. One was recorded on camera capturing and attempting to eat a hummingbird.

THE DARWIN'S BARK SPIDER MAKES ITS WEB OUT OF SILK THAT IS 10 TIMES STRONGER THAN KEVLAR, A MATERIAL USED TO MAKE BULLETPROOF VESTS AND COMBAT HELMETS.

The claws of coconut crabs can pinch with the greatest force of any **CRUSTACEAN** in the world. Their claws are stronger than the bite force of most bears!

The **RHINOCEROS BEETLE** can lift an object more than 800 times its own weight. That's like a human lifting an adult blue whale!

THE LARGEST AND THE SMALLEST

THE **ATLAS MOTH** IS THE LARGEST MOTH IN THE WORLD. IT IS BIGGER THAN AN ADULT HUMAN'S HAND.

The *Patu digua* is the smallest species of spider in the world. It is small enough to stand on the tip of a needle!

FAIRY FLIES AND HAIRY WINGED BEETLES ARE SOME OF THE SMALLEST INSECTS IN THE WORLD. THEY ARE SMALLER THAN THE TIP OF A PENCIL.

A **LEAF MINER LARVA** is so small that it spends its entire larval stage eating a tiny area of a single leaf.

THE *TEMNOTHORAX CRASSISPINUS* ANT IS SO TINY THAT THE ENTIRE COLONY CAN LIVE INSIDE A SINGLE HOLLOW ACORN.

Ants are small, but what they lack in size, they make up for in population. There are 10 QUADRILLION ants on the planet at any given moment. That's 1.4 million ants for every human!

UNDERWATER ADVENTURERS

THE RIFFLE BEETLE LIVES ITS ENTIRE LIFE UNDERWATER. IT ENCASES ITSELF IN A LAYER OF AIR CALLED A PLASTRON, SO IT NEVER HAS TO RESURFACE FOR AIR.

Scientists believe that *Polyrhachis sokolova* is the only species of ant that can live underwater.

WATER BOATMEN ARE A TYPE OF TRUE BUG THAT BREATHE UNDER-WATER BY STORING WATER AROUND THEIR BODIES.

A COCKROACH CAN HOLD ITS BREATH FOR 40 MINUTES WHILE UNDERWATER!

To dive underwater, some beetles carry the oxygen they need in bubbles attached to their bodies.

The **NYMPHS** (young insects) of dragonflies, caddis flies, mayflies, and stone flies breathe underwater using gills.

DID YOU HEAR THAT?

KATYDIDS HAVE THE SMALLEST EARS OF ANY ANIMAL, BUT THESE TINY EARS ALLOW THEM TO DETECT PREDATORS, FIND MATES, AND DISCOVER FOOD.

LOBSTERS can hear and produce sound, but they don't have ears. Instead of hearing sounds the way we do, they **"FEEL"** sounds through the vibration of water.

The **PRAYING MANTIS** has only one ear, located on the underside of its belly.

LACEWINGS have ears on their wings. When their small ears sense a bat nearby, they fold their wings and dive to avoid being caught.

THE EARS OF MOSQUITOES AND FRUIT FLIES ARE LOCATED ON THEIR ANTENNAE. MALE MOSQUITOES CAN HEAR THE WING FLAPS OF FEMALES FROM UP TO 32 FEET (10 METERS) AWAY!

The **BLADDER GRASSHOPPER** has six pairs of ears along its abdomen.

YOUR ANTENNAE ARE SHOWING

SOME CRUSTACEAN LARVAE KNOWN AS NAUPLIUS USE THEIR FIRST PAIR OF ANTENNAE TO SWIM.

Insect antennae have three basic parts: the SCAPE, the PEDICEL, and the FLAGELLOMERES.

Insects use their ANTENNAE to smell the world around them, to feel the surfaces of objects, and to detect the movement of wind.

CRUSTACEANS HAVE TWO PAIRS OF ANTENNAE.

SOMETHING SMELLS!

CRABS FLICK THEIR ANTENNAE TO CREATE WIND CURRENTS THAT RUN ACROSS TINY HAIRS ON THEIR ANTENNAE AND ALLOW THEM TO SMELL.

SPIDERS SMELL USING SCENT-SENSITIVE HAIRS ON THEIR LEGS.

MOSQUITOES use their antennae to sniff out chemicals in human sweat when looking for a meal.

MALE GIANT SILK MOTHS CAN SMELL A FEMALE MOTH FROM 7 MILES (11 KM) AWAY.

SENDING MESSAGES

MOST INSECTS COMMUNICATE WITH OTHERS OF THEIR KIND ONLY DURING MATING. OTHERWISE, THEY DON'T COMMUNICATE WITH ONE ANOTHER.

To communicate, male **TREEHOPPERS** emit a thrumming sound from their abdomen that sends vibrations down their legs and along the stems of leaves to other insects.

Tree crickets rub their wings together to create chirping noises to communicate.

LET'S EAT!

BEETLE LARVAE ARE N'T PICKY EATERS—THEY CAN ACT AS HERBIVORES BY EATING PLANTS, SCAVENGERS BY FINDING FOOD, OR PREDATORS BY EATING OTHER INSECTS.

PRAYING MANTISES use their powerful front legs to swiftly grasp prey and hold it while they eat.

Once a tick has found a suitable host, like a deer or a mouse, it uses its mouthparts to feed on the blood of the host.

Most spiders use their fangs to inject digestive enzymes into their prey, which allows them to eat the liquefied remains.

Some BEETLES are big enough to catch, kill, and eat tadpoles and smaller fish.

RECEPTORS OF ALL KINDS

ATLAS MOTHS ARE COVERED IN TINY HAIRS THAT SEND NERVE SIGNALS TO THEIR BRAINS WHENEVER THE HAIRS ARE MOVED. THIS HELPS THEM AVOID PREDATORS AND DETECT CHANGES IN WEATHER.

Insects have **BARORECEPTORS**, which allow them to determine changes in pressure and detect changes in weather.

THERMORECEPTORS allow insects to detect changes in temperature, which helps the insects avoid getting too hot or too cold.

INSECTS HAVE PROPRIOCEPTORS, WHICH SEND OUT NERVE SIGNALS THAT HELP THEM IDENTIFY THE POSITIONS OF THEIR LEGS, ANTENNAE, AND OTHER BODY PARTS.

RECEPTORS are tools that help bugs sense the environment around them. The basic receptors of insects are small hairs or larger bristles known as setae.

Chapter 3

IT'S A BUG'S LIFE

BUGS **REPRODUCE** QUICKLY, BUT NOT ALL BUGS REPRODUCE THE SAME WAY. SOME REPRODUCE ONLY AT CERTAIN TIMES OF THE YEAR. OTHERS REPRODUCE RANDOMLY THROUGHOUT THE YEAR.

THE CYCLE OF LIFE

BUTTERFLIES AND **MOTHS** EXPERIENCE COMPLETE METAMORPHOSIS BECAUSE THEY HAVE A COCOON STAGE, SIMILAR TO A PUPA STAGE.

COMPLETE METAMORPHOSIS HAS FOUR STAGES: EGG, LARVA, PUPA, AND ADULT.

THRIPS go through incomplete metamorphosis because they don't have a pupa stage. The **PUPA** is what develops after a young insect wraps itself in a silky cocoon.

There are two types of insect life cycles: COMPLETE METAMORPHOSIS and INCOMPLETE METAMORPHOSIS.

INCOMPLETE METAMORPHOSIS HAS THREE STAGES: EGG, NYMPH, AND ADULT.

COOL COCOONS

THE TERSA SPHINX MOTH BUILDS ITS COCOON ON THE SURFACE OF SOIL OR JUST BELOW IT.

The **BORNEAN CATERPILLAR** builds its cocoon completely out of poisonous tree resin instead of silk.

Insects that build cocoons can pause growth when environmental conditions are harmful. This is called DORMANCY. The pupae are protected in the safety of their cocoons and emerge as adults when conditions are better.

SOME ANT LARVAE SPIN COCOONS TO PROTECT THEMSELVES FROM PREDATORS AND DISEASES.

Adult female **BAGWORM MOTHS** love their cocoons so much that they never leave them. They reinforce their silky cocoons with twigs and leaves to help keep predators out.

LOVE BUGS

A male **PRAYING MANTIS** puts on elaborate dance displays to impress a female.

A male **SCORPION FLY** brings a gift of food to a female before mating. The feast will help nourish the eggs she is preparing to lay.

Male **MANDOLIN MOTHS** use their back wings to make music to charm females during mating season.

SOAPBERRY BUGS STAY CONNECTED TO THEIR PARTNERS FOR UP TO 11 DAYS DURING MATING.

STICK BUGS AND COCKROACHES CAN PRODUCE OFFSPRING ON THEIR OWN, WITHOUT MATING! THIS IS CALLED PARTHENOGENESIS.

THE BEST NESTS

SPINIFEX TERMITES BUILD CATHEDRAL-LIKE MOUND NESTS OUT OF CLAY AND SAND. ONE OF THESE MOUNDS CAN WEIGH MORE THAN AN ELEPHANT!

WEAVER ANTS BUILD NESTS BY WEAVING TOGETHER LEAVES HIGH IN THE CANOPY OF TREES. THEY USE THE SILK OF LARVAE LIKE GLUE TO HOLD LEAVES TOGETHER.

MEADOW SPITTLEBUGS make their nests out of "SPIT" that they produce with their bottoms!

To make a nest, the **MASON BEE** digs a hole and lines the inside of it with flower petals and moist soil.

77

EGG-LAYING INSECTS

THE GIANT ICHNEUMON WASP HAS THE LONGEST OVIPOSITOR OF ANY WASP AT ROUGHLY 5½ INCHES (142 MM) LONG. THAT'S LONGER THAN AN IPHONE!

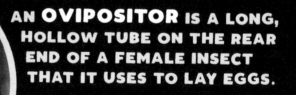

AN OVIPOSITOR IS A LONG, HOLLOW TUBE ON THE REAR END OF A FEMALE INSECT THAT IT USES TO LAY EGGS.

The CLISTOPYGA WASP uses its ovipositor to sting spiders and lay its eggs in the spider.

THE OVIPOSITORS OF FEMALE BEES HAVE **EVOLVED** TO BECOME STINGING TOOLS. ONLY THE QUEEN BEE USES HER OVIPOSITOR TO LAY EGGS.

No living **MAYFLY** species has an ovipositor, but through studying fossils, it's believed that their ancestors did!

Some species of wasp use their **OVIPOSITORS** to drill into tree bark and lay their eggs inside grubs beneath the bark.

EGG-CELLENT EGGS

MALE DAMSELFLIES BELLY-FLOP INTO THE WATER TO LET THE FEMALE KNOW THAT THEY'VE FOUND A GREAT PLACE TO LAY EGGS.

CARPENTER BEES produce the largest eggs in the insect world.

FRUIT FLIES can lay up to 500 eggs at a time.

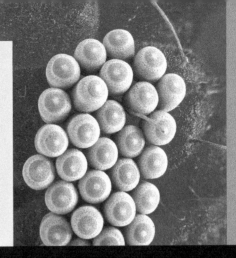

STINK BUGS CAN CHOOSE THE COLOR OF THEIR EGGS IN ORDER TO HIDE THEM FROM PREDATORS. THE EGGS CAN BE PALE YELLOW TO BLACK, DEPENDING ON THE COLOR OF THE SURFACE ON WHICH THEY'RE LAID.

The eggs of stink bugs have little blobs of nutrients on top of them that attract ants. This motivates the ants to carry the eggs off to the safety of their colony, where they store the eggs until they hatch.

The **QUEEN TERMITE** of the species *Belicositermes natalensis* lays about 1,250 eggs per hour. That's 10 million eggs in one year, and she may live up to 20 or even 50 years!

ARTHROPOD TEAMWORK

SOLDIER TERMITES HAVE HUGE, SHARP MOUTHPARTS THAT THEY USE TO DEFEND THEMSELVES AGAINST PREDATORS.

To protect themselves from giant hornets, **JAPANESE HONEYBEES** can use their bodies to form a ball around the hornet and vibrate their flight muscles, creating heat. The bees can survive the rise in temperature, but the hornet cannot.

Anelosimus eximius spiders work together to build some of the largest webs in the world, up to 25 feet long (7.6 m) and 5 feet wide (1.5 m).

During intense floods, FIRE ANTS link together to form a floating raft. They can float like this for weeks without drowning.

WITHIN A COUPLE OF HOURS, A SMALL GROUP OF GIANT HORNETS CAN KILL AND EAT THOUSANDS OF BEES IN A COLONY.

Both MONARCHS and LOCUSTS work together with their own kind to migrate, or move from one place to another, in swarms. Traveling in swarms increases their ability to survive long journeys.

83

STARTLING SPIDERLINGS

BABY SPIDERS
ARE CALLED SPIDERLINGS.

Female WOLF SPIDERS lay dozens of eggs at a time, wrap them in a silky sac, and carry them on their backs. After the eggs hatch, the mother carries the spiderlings for several more days!

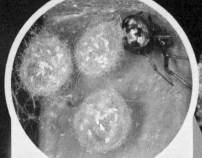

COMB-FOOTED SPIDERS feed their spiderlings liquid from their mouths.

SPIDERLINGS DON'T HAVE WINGS, BUT MANY CAN FLY AS HIGH AS BIRDS BY USING THEIR SILK TO MAKE "PARACHUTES" THAT FLOAT THROUGH THE AIR. THIS IS CALLED BALLOONING.

DESERT SPIDERS stop eating after their spiderlings hatch. Over the next few weeks, the mother regurgitates old meals to feed her hungry spiderlings!

YOU'RE GETTING SLEEPY . . .

SOME SPECIES OF COCKROACHES FOLD DOWN THEIR ANTENNAE TO PROTECT THEM WHEN THEY SLEEP.

Insects sleep, but they don't have eyelids, so they can't close their eyes to sleep like humans do.

WHEN INSECTS SLEEP OR REST, IT IS KNOWN AS TORPOR.

MIGRATING MONARCHS CLUMP TOGETHER AND SLEEP IN ENORMOUS GROUPS. SLUMBER PARTY ANYONE?

Some scientists have discovered that sleep-deprived fruit flies have a harder time finding their way out of mazes than well-rested fruit flies.

BEES use their powerful JAWS to clamp down on a plant and dangle from it for hours while they sleep.

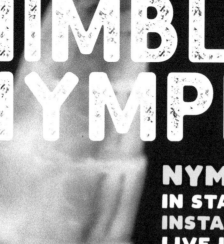

NIMBLE NYMPHS

NYMPHS GROW IN STAGES CALLED **INSTARS** AND OFTEN LIVE IN WATER, EVEN IF THE ADULT INSECTS DO NOT.

Some species of MAYFLY NYMPHS stay in this early stage of development for three to four years.

HEMIMETABOLOUS insects are insects that do not make cocoons. Baby hemimetabolous insects are called **NYMPHS**.

Many mayfly nymphs have flattened bodies that allow them to live in fast-flowing waters. The water glides over their flat bodies so they don't get swept away by the current.

LOTS OF LARVAE

HOLOMETABOLOUS INSECTS ARE INSECTS THAT MAKE COCOONS. THE LARVAE OF HOLOMETABOLOUS INSECTS LOOK NOTHING LIKE THE ADULTS. FOR EXAMPLE, A CATERPILLAR LOOKS NOTHING LIKE A BUTTERFLY.

Some LACEWING LARVAE camouflage themselves by attaching the dead bodies of their prey to spines along their back.

THE LARVAE OF SPONGILLAFLIES DEVELOP INSIDE OF AND FEED ON FRESHWATER SPONGES! THEY USE THEIR LONG MOUTHPARTS TO PIERCE THE SPONGE'S CELLS AND CONSUME IT SLOWLY.

ANTLION LARVAE do not have complete digestive systems. Waste builds up in their guts until it is released at the end of their pupal stage.

BEAUTIFUL BUTTERFLIES

WHILE A CATERPILLAR IS INSIDE ITS COCOON, IT IS CALLED A PUPA.

After mating, female butterflies choose very specific plants to lay their eggs on. They can recognize different plants by their shapes and colors.

BUTTERFLIES CAN RECOGNIZE INDIVIDUALS OF THEIR OWN SPECIES BY IDENTIFYING THE COLORS AND PATTERNS ON THEIR WINGS.

The males of some species of butterflies do courtship "DANCES" and release special chemicals into the air to attract females.

During complete metamorphosis, caterpillars build cocoons and stay inside them for a few weeks, months, or sometimes even years.

BUTTERFLY BABYSITTERS

FOR NINE MONTHS OUT OF THE YEAR, THE ALCON BLUE BUTTERFLY ALLOWS ITS BABIES TO BE RAISED BY OTHER INSECTS.

The **ALCON BLUE LARVA** releases a sweet substance that *Myrmica* ants like to eat. After an ant eats the substance, it will adopt the larva and take it back to its nest.

THE *MYRMICA* ANTS WILL CONTINUE TO FEED THE ALCON BLUE LARVA INSTEAD OF THEIR OWN, WHICH MAY LEAD TO THE ANT COLONY PRODUCING FEWER OFFSPRING.

The Alcon blue caterpillar will spend up to 23 months underground with the ant colony before finally pupating.

When the Alcon blue emerges from its cocoon as a butterfly, the ants immediately attack it, but it is protected by scales covering its body.

MAYFLY MAYHEM

BOTH MALE AND FEMALE MAYFLIES HAVE TWO SETS OF REPRODUCTIVE ORGANS.

Mayflies have a unique developmental stage called the SUBIMAGO stage. During this stage the mayfly can use its wings and looks like an adult, but it is still too young to mate.

Scientists use mayflies to help determine water quality. Mayflies can only survive in clean, unpolluted water.

Several species of fish, frogs, and birds rely on mayflies as a food source. Many animals would become endangered without mayflies to eat.

MAYFLY NYMPHS SPEND AN ENTIRE YEAR IN FRESH WATER. WHEN THEY FINALLY EMERGE AS ADULTS, MOST SPECIES OF MAYFLY LIVE FOR ONLY ONE DAY.

Adult mayflies do not have functioning mouthparts and can't eat!

PLANET OF THE ANTS

NOT ALL ANT EGGS MAKE IT TO ADULTHOOD. SOMETIMES NEST MATES WILL EAT NEARBY EGGS FOR EXTRA NOURISHMENT.

MALE ANTS HAVE WINGS AND USUALLY FLY TO MATE WITH QUEENS. THEY NEVER DO ANY CHORES WITHIN THE COLONY AND USUALLY LIVE FOR ONLY A FEW WEEKS.

Ants go through complete metamorphosis, just like butterflies. First they are eggs, then hungry larvae, and then they pupate before finally emerging as an adult males or females.

In most species of ants, the workers are females that were underfed as larvae and do not reproduce as adults.

QUEENS are female ants that were overfed as larvae. When the conditions are right, they can live for decades.

LET'S TALK LIFE SPANS

CICADAS LIVE FOR ABOUT FIVE WEEKS ABOVEGROUND WHILE LOOKING FOR MATES. HOWEVER, BEFORE CICADAS BECOME ADULTS, THEY SPEND 2 TO 17 YEARS UNDERGROUND AS LARVAE.

Most BLACK WIDOW SPIDER live for one year after reaching maturity, but some can live for up to two years.

Adult BEDBUGS can live for four to six months and can go weeks or even months without food.

AMERICAN COCKROACHES CAN LIVE FOR A YEAR IF THEY HAVE ENOUGH FOOD TO EAT.

SPLENDOUR BEETLES CAN REMAIN IN THE LARVA STAGE FOR UP TO 30 YEARS.

Chapter 4

HOMES AND HABITATS

BUGS OCCUPY NEARLY EVERY CORNER OF EARTH. OVER MILLIONS OF YEARS, THEY HAVE ADAPTED TO LIVE AND THRIVE IN SOME OF THE HARSHEST AND MOST EXTREME ENVIRONMENTS IN THE WORLD.

HOME ALONE . . . WITH BUGS

Every home has an average of 100 different species of bugs living in it. That's a lot of diversity right under our roofs!

CARPENTER ANTS BURROW INTO THE WOOD OF HOUSES AND BUILD NESTS.

CARPET BEETLES LIKE TO LIVE IN THE CARPETS OF OUR HOMES. THEY ALSO LIKE TO CHILL INSIDE FOLDED CLOTHES, DRAWERS, AND CLOSETS.

The **GERMAN COCKROACH** is the type we most often see in our homes. They love dark, damp places so you'll usually find them hiding in the kitchen and bathroom.

CENTIPEDES MAY LOOK SCARY, BUT THEY KEEP OTHER CREEPY-CRAWLIES OUT OF OUR HOMES. THEY HUNT COCKROACHES, SPIDERS, AND BEETLE LARVAE.

SILVERFISH ARE USUALLY BROUGHT INTO HOMES ON CARDBOARD BOXES. THEY EAT A VARIETY OF THINGS, FROM CEREAL AND FLOUR TO BOOKS AND GLUE!

105

BACKYARD BUGS

DURING THE WINTER, WHITE GRUBS BURROW INTO SOIL IN THE GROUND TO AVOID FREEZING. THEY CAN STAY BURIED FOR MONTHS!

SOD WEBWORMS are not worms at all, but small moths that can be seen flying in zigzag patterns whenever the grass is mowed.

CUTWORMS LIVE IN BURROWS IN THE YARD AND USUALLY EMERGE ONLY AT NIGHT TO MUNCH ON THE GRASS.

An adult CHINCH BUG is about the size of the tip of a pencil. They love munching on the grass in your lawn.

BILLBUGS ARE WEEVILS THAT LOVE HIDING IN THE LEAF LITTER IN YOUR YARD. IN THE SPRING THEY LAY THEIR EGGS INSIDE BLADES OF GRASS.

APHIDS, ALSO KNOWN AS "PLANT LICE," LOVE THE SUCCULENT LEAVES IN YOUR GARDEN.

STOP BUGGING ME!

SOME MITES
LIVE ON THE
SKIN OF HORSES
AND FEED ON
THE HORSES'
SKIN CELLS.

BOTFLIES lay their eggs under the skin of various mammals (hosts). The larva grows and develops beneath the skin of the host and emerges when ready to pupate. The host heals afterward.

TICKS LIVE IN MOIST, SHADY AREAS AND CLING TO TALL GRASSES WAITING FOR AN ANIMAL TO PASS BY. IF AN ANIMAL PASSES BY CLOSELY ENOUGH, THE TICK WILL ATTACH TO THE ANIMAL AND LIVE BURIED IN ITS FUR.

LIVING UNDER A ROCK

SOME SPECIES OF RED ANTS BUILD NESTS THAT ARE ALMOST INVISIBLE UNDER LARGE ROCKS!

CRICKETS love living beneath rocks, especially if the rocks are covered in delicious fungi and surrounded by tasty decaying plants.

THE AREA UNDER A ROCK MAY NOT SEEM INTERESTING, BUT MANY INSECTS CALL THIS DARK SPACE HOME. THESE SPACES ARE CALLED **MICROHABITATS**, WHICH ARE SMALL AREAS THAT ARE PART OF A MUCH BIGGER ECOSYSTEM.

DURING THE HARSH WINTER MONTHS, LADYBIRD BEETLES GATHER IN GROUPS OF 50 TO 100 AND CUDDLE TOGETHER BENEATH ROCKS TO KEEP WARM!

Wood lice, also known as **"ROLY-POLIES,"** can spend the majority of their lives in the dark, cool environment under a rock.

AQUATIC HOMES

CRAYFISH LIVE IN PONDS, STREAMS, RIVERS, AND LAKES. THEY DIG BURROWS BENEATH LOGS OR ROCKS SUBMERGED IN STREAMS, AND SOME SPECIES EVEN BUILD LARGE MUD TOWERS WHEN DIGGING TUNNELS.

AQUATIC WORMS live at the bottom of streams, buried beneath the wet sand. They graze on bacteria and algae that settle there.

GIANT WATER BUGS live in freshwater ponds, marshy areas, and slow-moving pools in streams. They love to hide in thick plants just under the surface of the water.

DIVING BELL SPIDERS LIVE ALMOST ENTIRELY UNDERWATER. TO BREATHE, THEY USE THEIR WEB TO CREATE A DOME THAT TRAPS OXYGEN.

DOBSONFLY LARVAE live in swift-flowing waters in stream habitats. They prefer to live under big rocks where they are safe from predators and won't be swept away.

RIFFLE BEETLES live in areas of a stream where riffles, or small waves, are present. The beetles have claws that help them cling to smooth rocks in the water.

MIGRATORS
ON THE MOVE

EACH SPRING, AROUND HALF A BILLION HOVERFLIES ARRIVE IN SOUTHERN ENGLAND. THIS MASSIVE MIGRATION ALLOWS THE HOVERFLIES TO FIND THE BEST FOOD AND HABITAT CONDITIONS.

Common green darners are migrating dragonflies. They migrate south during fall and early winter to breed and lay their eggs.

THE MONARCH IS THE ONLY BUTTERFLY KNOWN TO MAKE A TWO-WAY MIGRATION. MONARCHS CANNOT SURVIVE NORTHERN WINTERS, SO THEY FLY ALMOST 3,000 MILES (4,828 KM) SOUTH, WHERE IT IS WARMER.

ON AUSTRALIA'S CHRISTMAS ISLAND, 40 MILLION TO 50 MILLION RED CRABS MIGRATE FROM THE JUNGLE TO THE SEA. THE PEOPLE ON THE ISLAND CLOSE ROADS AND BUILD BRIDGES TO HELP THE CRABS TRAVEL SAFELY.

Spiders don't typically migrate, but in 2021, Australia experienced extreme storms and flooding, and millions of spiders used their webs to create parachutes to fly to safety.

LOCUSTS usually like to be alone, but warm weather prompts them to swarm and migrate to find new food sources.

BUGS AT THE EXTREMES

LAVA CRICKETS ARE THE ONLY MULTICELLULAR LIFE-FORM THAT LIVES ON THE BRITTLE SURFACE OF COOLING LAVA.

FLAT BARK BEETLES live in Alaska and have special chemicals, known as antifreeze proteins, in their bodies that keep them from freezing.

The **ANTARCTIC MIDGE** is the only insect that lives in Antarctica. Scientists believe that its underground home is slightly warmer, helping it survive in one of the coldest places on Earth!

EXTREMOPHILES are animals that can live and thrive in extreme conditions that humans typically would not survive.

Adult **BRINE FLIES** live in extremely salty water. They lay their eggs in the water and feed on algae that live there.

SAND WASPS LIVE IN SOUTHERN DESERTS WHERE TEMPERATURES RANGE FROM 100°F TO 120°F (38°C TO 49°C).

UNDER ONE ROOF

SOME SPECIES OF ANTS BUILD THEIR NESTS UNDERGROUND. THEY HAVE SEPARATE ROOMS FOR WASTE AND FOOD AND STILL HAVE SPACE IN THEIR NESTS TO HOUSE AROUND 500,000 ANTS!

BUMBLEBEES live in small colonies with anywhere from 50 to 500 individuals. They nest in rocky holes or grassy hollows, and sometimes they'll occupy old nests made by mice or birds.

HORNETS BUILD THE BIGGEST NESTS OF ALL WASPS! A HORNET NEST CAN BE AS BIG AS A BASKETBALL, AND AROUND 25,000 HORNETS CAN LIVE IN ONE NEST.

TERMITES usually nest underground, but some termites build their nests in trees from tiny fibers of wood that they mix with spit.

119

TERMITE TOWERS

IN AUSTRALIA, TERMITES BUILD CATHEDRAL-LIKE MOUNDS THAT CAN STAND FOR UP TO 100 YEARS. THAT'S SOME SERIOUS ENGINEERING!

Amitermes meridionalis termites build mounds that are always turned in a certain direction. Scientists believe this placement helps with cooling and heating the mound when outside temperatures change.

TERMITE MOUNDS HAVE SEVERAL CHAMBERS OR ROOMS. THEY HAVE PANTRIES TO STORE FOOD, INDOOR GARDENS FOR GROWING EDIBLE FUNGI, AND A NURSERY FOR EGGS.

African termites build umbrella-shaped mounds that can withstand heavy rainfall.

Temperatures may reach 100°F (38°C) outside a termite mound, but the mound maintains a constant temperature inside because termites build tunnels and chimneys to create airflow.

DUNG DWELLINGS

FLESH FLIES BREED AND LAY THEIR EGGS IN FRESH DUNG. THE LARVAE OF FLESH FLIES FEED ON THE DUNG FOR THREE TO FOUR DAYS BEFORE ENTERING THE PUPAL STAGE.

DUNG BEETLES FILL THEIR BURROW WITH HUGE BALLS OF DUNG OR WASTE. THE BEETLES USE THE DUNG AS A HOME FOR THEIR EGGS, AS WELL AS FOR FOOD.

"SCATOPHAGOUS" is a word used to describe insects that feed on dung.

DAMPWOOD TERMITES USE THEIR OWN DUNG TO BUILD UP THEIR NESTS.

HERBIVOROUS BEETLE LARVAE ARE SMALL AND SLOW, AND THEY LIVE IN THE DANGEROUS OPEN CANOPY OF TREES. TO AVOID BEING EATEN, HERBIVOROUS BEETLE LARVAE BUILD "FECAL SHIELDS" ON THEIR BACKS, MADE FROM THEIR OWN WASTE.

COZY CAVES

THE *META MENARDI SPIDER* TAKES ADVANTAGE OF DARK CAVES. IT SPINS ITS WEB IN SHADOWY CORNERS OF A CAVE, MAKING THE WEB DIFFICULT FOR OTHER BUGS TO SEE OR AVOID.

The **KENTUCKY CAVE SHRIMP** has no eyes. You can see right through its translucent body!

TROGLOBITIC beetles have adapted to living in the darkness of caves. They can't see, but their senses of touch, hearing, and smell are excellent.

In Malaysia, in Southeast Asia, cockroaches fill the Gomantong Cave and survive by eating bat feces.

The *Cryptops speleorex* centipede is called the "KING OF THE CAVE" in Romania. The caves where these centipedes are found are low in oxygen and thick in toxic gases.

VELVET WORMS ARE SOFT-BODIED CARNIVORES THAT LOVE DARK, DAMP CAVES. THEY USE THEIR LONG ANTENNAE TO FEEL AROUND WHEN HUNTING FOR FOOD IN COMPLETE DARKNESS.

IT'S HOT IN HERE!

INSECTS HAVE MANY WAYS TO SURVIVE THE HEAT. SOME COME OUT AT NIGHT; OTHERS HIDE IN THE SHADE OR DIG BURROWS DEEP UNDERGROUND. SOME HAVE SPECIAL PROTEINS TO KEEP THEIR BODIES FUNCTIONING WHEN TEMPERATURES GET TOO HIGH.

The **DARKLING BEETLE** stays cool in the desert heat by lifting its body and some of its feet off the ground.

FIRE BEETLES HAVE SPECIAL SENSORS ON THEIR BODIES THAT CAN DETECT HEAT. THEY FLY TOWARD FIRES TO LAY THEIR EGGS IN BURNED OR DAMAGED TREES.

SMOKE FLIES love hanging out near plumes of smoke from burning trees—they even lay their eggs in the soil near burned trees.

DESERT CRICKETS DIG HOLES IN THE HOT DESERT SAND USING SHORT, SPINE-COVERED LEGS. THESE LITTLE CRICKETS SURVIVE IN SWELTERING HEAT BY DRINKING MOISTURE THAT CONDENSES ON PLANTS.

FEMALE COCHINEAL INSECTS DO NOT HAVE WINGS OR LEGS. THEY LIVE ON THE SURFACE OF PRICKLY PEAR CACTI FOR THEIR ENTIRE LIVES.

127

RAIN FOREST RESIDENTS

THE COMET MOTH IS FOUND ONLY IN THE RAIN FOREST OF MADAGASCAR. IT HAS EYELIKE MARKINGS ON ITS WINGS TO SCARE AWAY PREDATORS.

The *Bombus transversalis* bumblebee lives underground in the Amazon rain forest. It builds a protective dome over its home, and sometimes as many as five bumblebees guard the entrance.

TWENTY-FIVE PERCENT OF ALL THE WORLD'S INSECT SPECIES LIVE IN THE CANOPY OF THE RAIN FOREST.

BULLET ANTS ARE FOUND IN LOWLAND RAIN FOREST AREAS AND BUILD NESTS AT THE BOTTOM OF TREES. THEY ARE KNOWN FOR THEIR PAINFUL BITE!

The *Cithaerias pireta*, also known as the "**BLUSHING PHANTOM**," is a butterfly with clear wings. These phantoms live deep within rain forest vegetation and are active at sunset.

TRIGONA SPINIPES is a stingless bee found in the Brazilian rain forest. Because it builds its nest in dung, its honey is not eaten by humans.

BUGS ON ICE

THE **AQUATIC LARVAE** OF WINTER STONE FLIES CLIMB ONTO THE SURFACE OF THE SNOW TO COMPLETE DEVELOPMENT AND BECOME ADULTS. ALTHOUGH WINTER STONE FLIES HAVE WINGS, THEY NORMALLY WALK ALONG THE SNOW TO FIND A MATE.

Grylloblattids, also known as **"ICE CRAWLERS,"** live in extremely cold habitats such as snowcapped mountains or ice caves.

SNOW CRICKETS live on mountaintops and the edges of glaciers. That's a serious case of cold feet!

FLIES ARE THE MOST COMMON OF ALL BUGS FOUND IN THE ARCTIC CIRCLE.

Arctic Circle

Dalton Highway   ALASKA   Latitude 66 33'

SNOW FLEAS are wingless insects found in the Sierra Nevada mountains. They are predatory insects that feed on other insects they hunt in snowy fields.

131

TOXIC HOMES

YETI CRABS

LIVE IN THE TOXIC WATERS CREATED BY HYDROTHERMAL VENTS, WHICH ARE OPENINGS IN THE SEA FLOOR WHERE HEAT AND MINERAL-RICH WATERS FLOW.

BLACKFLY LARVAE survive in extremely polluted water. Scientists use blackflies to determine whether a body of water is healthy or not. If a large population of blackfly larvae are present, then the water is polluted.

SULFURIC ACID IS STRONG ENOUGH TO BURN HOLES IN YOUR CLOTHES. BUT A SPECIES OF WORM KNOWN AS *LIMNODRILUS SULPHURENSIS* LIVES IN SULFUR GAS—FILLED CAVES. THESE RED WORMS SURVIVE BY EATING SULFUR-OXIDIZING BACTERIA.

IN 2012, SCIENTISTS DISCOVERED THE EYELESS SHRIMP *RIMICARIS HYBISAE*. THESE SHRIMP, LIKE YETI CRABS, LIVE IN TOXIC WATERS CREATED BY HYDROTHERMAL VENTS AND SURVIVE BY EATING GARDENS OF BACTERIA GROWING ON THEIR BODIES.

HIDDEN HOMES

TRAPDOOR SPIDERS LIVE IN BURROWS WITH TRAPDOORS THAT THE SPIDERS MAKE OUT OF LEAVES, SOIL, AND SILK.

WALKING STICKS resemble twigs and branches. Blending in with the trees they live in makes it hard for predators to spot them.

TURRET SPIDERS are ambush predators that build their burrows in trees. The spider feels the vibrations of nearby insects and lunges at its prey from the burrow when the moment is right.

LEAF INSECTS SPEND A LOT OF TIME STANDING PERFECTLY STILL TO TRICK PREDATORS INTO THINKING THEY ARE LEAVES. SOME EVEN MOVE THEIR BODIES TO LOOK LIKE LEAVES SWAYING IN THE WIND.

Chapter 5
POWERFUL PREDATORS

INSECTS MIGHT BE SMALL, BUT THEY CAN ALSO BE SKILLED **PREDATORS**! MANY BUGS, LIKE DRAGONFLIES AND DAMSELFLIES, ARE POWERFUL, WELL-ADAPTED HUNTERS.

FIGHTING BUGS

MALE GIRAFFE WEEVILS USE THEIR LONG NECKS TO FIGHT ONE ANOTHER!

Wheel bugs, also known as "ASSASSIN BUGS," have long, fang-like mouthparts that they use to stab and attack other insects.

FEMALE **FIREFLIES** SOMETIMES FLASH THEIR LIGHTS TO TRICK MALES INTO COMING CLOSER. WHEN THE MALE APPROACHES, THE FEMALE ATTACKS AND EATS HIM! BY EATING THE MALE, THE FEMALE INGESTS A TOXIN THAT PROTECTS HER FROM PREDATORS.

If another bug comes into their territory, leaf-footed bugs use their back legs to kick the intruder. These fights last from a few minutes to several hours.

The males of some species of BUTTERFLIES have intense battles in the sky during mating season. These battles can result in injuries, including ripped wings.

TACHINID FLIES LAY THEIR EGGS INSIDE OTHER INSECTS, BUT THE LARVAE DON'T LIKE TO SHARE THEIR SPACE. AFTER THE EGGS HATCH, THE LARVAE FIGHT ONE ANOTHER UNTIL ONLY ONE LARVA REMAINS.

BEETLE BATTLE!

Male **STAG BEETLES** use their mouthparts for battle. A bigger stag beetle will attempt to grab and lift a smaller stag beetle and crush it with its massive jaws.

TUNNELER BEETLES FIGHT ONE-ON ONE IN THEIR UNDERGROUND TUNNELS BY RAMMING THEIR HORNS INTO EACH OTHER.

THE JAPANESE RHINOCEROS BEETLE HAS A HUGE HORN STICKING OUT OF ITS HEAD, WHICH IT USES TO DEFEND ITS TERRITORY.

DUNG BEETLES OFTEN FIGHT OVER BALLS OF DUNG. SEVERAL BEETLES MAY SCRAMBLE AROUND EACH OTHER TRYING TO THROW THE OTHERS OFF BALANCE.

DURING MATING SEASON, MALE HERCULES BEETLES WILL PICK UP OTHER MALES AND TRY TO SMASH THEM INTO THE GROUND!

ELEPHANT BEETLES are huge compared to other beetles. When two male elephant beetles want to mate with the same female, they battle with their horns.

SPINE TIME

THE BODIES OF SPINY KING CRABS, ALSO KNOWN AS "PORCUPINE CRABS," ARE ENTIRELY COVERED IN SPINES.

The caterpillar of the **BUCK MOTH** grows several branching spines with red or black tips. The spines keep the caterpillar safe until it is ready to pupate.

LIKE SPINY KING CRABS, SPINY LOBSTERS HAVE AN EXOSKELETON COVERED IN SPINES. THE SPINES PROVIDE SOME PROTECTION, BUT A HUNGRY NURSE SHARK WILL RISK BEING STABBED TO EAT A YUMMY SPINY LOBSTER.

THE SPINED SOLDIER BUG IS A STINK BUG WITH LARGE SPINES ON EACH SHOULDER. THESE SPINES SERVE AS A DEFENSE AGAINST PREDATORS.

SPINY-BACKED ORB WEAVER SPIDERS have several spines growing from their abdomen. Their bodies are round, and the spines prevent birds and lizards from catching the spiders in their mouths.

SPEARER MANTIS SHRIMP have between 2 and 20 sharp spines on their pincers. They use them to hunt prey and fight off predators.

CHEMICAL DEFENSES

ONLY A BRAVE PREDATOR WILL TRY TO EAT THE BOMBARDIER BEETLE. WHEN THREATENED, THE BOMBARDIER BEETLE SPRAYS BOILING-HOT LIQUID FROM ITS REAR END!

WHEN THREATENED, DARKLING BEETLES TILT THEIR HEADS DOWN AND THEIR TAILS UP TO RELEASE A STINKY, DARK LIQUID. IT WASHES OFF EASILY IF IT GETS ON YOU, BUT YOU WILL REMEMBER THE SMELL!

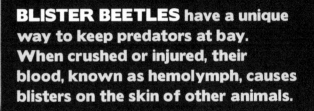

LEAF BEETLES PRODUCE TOXINS FROM THEIR SKIN TO DETER PREDATORS. THE LEAF BEETLE CAN PRODUCE THESE TOXINS THROUGHOUT ITS LIFETIME, EVEN AS AN EGG, LARVA, OR PUPA.

BLISTER BEETLES have a unique way to keep predators at bay. When crushed or injured, their blood, known as hemolymph, causes blisters on the skin of other animals.

The PIPEVINE SWALLOWTAIL BUTTERFLY and CATERPILLAR are poisonous to predators because they feed on a poisonous plant known as a pipevine.

SADDLEBACK CATERPILLARS have hollow hairs all over their bodies. These hairs can cause a burning feeling for hours if an animal brushes against them.

PINCHING PREDATORS

MALE **FIDDLER CRABS** HAVE ONE REGULAR CLAW AND ONE SUPER CLAW. THEY USE THE REGULAR CLAW TO PICK UP FOOD FROM THE BEACH, BUT SUPER-SIZED CLAW IS USED TO FIGHT.

TAILLESS WHIP SCORPIONS have two pincers that look like regular legs, but they aren't used for walking—they're used to quickly subdue prey.

Adult TIGER BEETLES hunt and run down their prey, catching it with their pincers.

EMPEROR SCORPIONS HAVE LARGE PINCERS WITH SENSORY HAIRS THAT HELP THEM FIND PREY BY DETECTING VIBRATIONS CAUSED BY MOVEMENT IN THE AIR.

PSEUDOSCORPIONS are related to spiders. Because they have bad eyesight, they use sensory hairs and their large pincers to find and catch prey.

EARWIGS HAVE PINCERS ON THEIR BOTTOMS. FEMALES HAVE STRAIGHT PINCERS, AND MALES HAVE CURVED PINCERS.

147

AN APPETITE FOR APHIDS

LADYBUG LARVAE CAN EACH EAT HUNDREDS OF APHIDS A DAY. GARDENERS OFTEN PUT LADYBUGS INTO THEIR GARDENS TO KEEP APHIDS FROM EATING THEIR PLANTS.

Green lacewings, also known as "**APHID LIONS,**" will eat just about any soft-bodied pest. They love munching on aphids.

ADULT HOVERFLIES LAY THEIR EGGS NEAR HUGE APHID COLONIES. WHEN THE LARVAE HATCH, IT IS AN ALL-YOU-CAN-EAT FEAST!

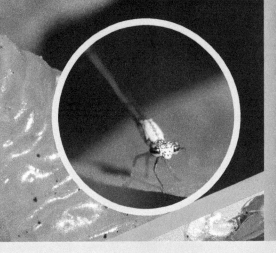

The *APHIDIUS COLEMANI WASP* is an extremely effective predator. Females can take over the bodies of as many as 300 aphids by laying eggs inside them.

APHID WASPS lay their eggs in dead plant stems and then pack the stems with aphids so their offspring can feed after hatching.

TINY PARASITIC WASPS LAY THEIR EGGS DIRECTLY INSIDE LIVING APHIDS.

VENOMOUS VERMIN

BOLAS SPIDERS USE THEIR WEBS LIKE FISHING LINES. THEY WHIRL THE WEB IN THE AIR WITH A STICKY BLOB ON ONE END THAT STICKS TO MOTHS FLYING BY.

SPITTING SPIDERS spit sticky venom over their prey so they can't escape!

THE **BLIND REMIPEDE** IS THE FIRST VENOMOUS CRUSTACEAN DISCOVERED BY SCIENTISTS. IT LIVES IN UNDERWATER CAVES AND HUNTS USING A VENOM SIMILAR TO THE VENOM FOUND IN RATTLESNAKES.

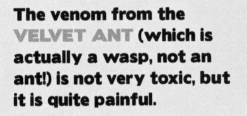

The venom from the **VELVET ANT** (which is actually a wasp, not an ant!) is not very toxic, but it is quite painful.

HARVESTER ANTS have the most toxic venom in the insect world. Unlike bees, harvester ants can sting over and over again. However, the venom of one ant isn't enough to kill a human.

The **SYDNEY FUNNEL-WEB SPIDER** builds webs and hides deep inside them. When an insect comes close, the spider jumps out, grabs it, and injects venom with its sharp fangs.

151

ITTY-BITTY BITERS

BROWN RECLUSE SPIDERS PACK A POWERFUL BITE! MOST ANIMALS DON'T EVEN FEEL IT WHEN THEY ARE FIRST BITTEN BY THE BROWN RECLUSE, BUT AFTER A FEW SECONDS THE PAIN INTENSIFIES AND SPREADS.

CHIGGERS, OR HARVEST MITES, ARE EXTREMELY SMALL. THEY LIKE TO HANG OUT NEAR TALL GRASSES AND WATERY AREAS UNTIL THEY CAN ATTACH TO OTHER ANIMALS AND BITE THEIR LEGS.

FLOWER CRAB SPIDERS WAIT INSIDE FLOWERS FOR INSECTS TO COME NEAR. IF AN INSECT APPROACHES THE FLOWER, THE CRAB SPIDER QUICKLY GRABS IT.

KISSING BUGS bite animals on the face and then poop near the wound.

DARING DANCERS

MANGROVE CRABS WAVE THEIR CLAWS UP AND DOWN AFTER DEFEATING AN ENEMY IN BATTLE. SCIENTISTS BELIEVE THAT THIS DANCE HELPS SCARE OFF FUTURE ATTACKERS.

To **WARN PREDATORS** away, beech aphids, also known as **"BOOGIE-WOOGIE"** aphids, put their bottoms in the air and vibrate them, sometimes shaking the branch they inhabit.

SOME SPECIES OF WASP DRUM THEIR ABDOMENS AGAINST DIFFERENT PARTS OF THEIR NEST TO SEND MESSAGES TO OTHER WASPS THAT FOOD IS NEARBY.

I'M A SURVIVOR!

NOT ALL INSECTS HAVE FANCY WEAPONRY. SOME RELY ON AGILITY AND SPEED TO AVOID BEING EATEN. SOME SPECIES OF FLIES CAN FLY AWAY ONLY 30 TO 50 MILLISECONDS AFTER SENSING A THREAT!

WHEN **DAPHNIA**, OR WATER FLEAS, SENSE DANGER NEARBY, THEY CAN GROW A HELMET OF SPIKES AND A TAIL-SPINE TO DETER PREDATORS.

CLICK BEETLES play dead to avoid being eaten. Whenever they are touched by a predator, they immediately stop moving and fall over on their backs.

Some insects mimic the appearance of a poisonous insect to keep predators away. The viceroy butterfly looks like a poisonous monarch. It's a win for the twin!

157

ODONATA
HUNTERS

ONE STUDY FOUND THAT FOUR
DIFFERENT SPECIES OF DRAGONFLIES
COULD CATCH AND EAT ALMOST
2 POUNDS (900 GRAMS) OF INSECTS
IN ONE SUMMER. THAT'S EQUIVALENT
TO 700,000 MEDIUM-SIZE MIDGES.

NEW RESEARCH SUGGESTS THAT DRAGONFLIES ARE SO SUCCESSFUL AT HUNTING BECAUSE THEY CAN LEARN HOW THEIR PREY BEHAVES AND PREDICT WHAT IT WILL DO.

IN 2013, A YOUTUBER CAPTURED A DRAGONFLY CATCHING A LIZARD ON VIDEO! DRAGONFLIES NORMALLY HUNT IN THE AIR, SO THIS BEHAVIOR WAS UNUSUAL.

DAMSELFLIES can eat hundreds of thousands of insects in a single summer.

Dragonflies and damselflies belong to the insect order *Odonata*, and they are some of the best predators in the animal kingdom. They catch 95 percent of all insects they target!

APHIDOLETE APPETITES

APHIDOLETES ARE A TYPE OF FLY WHOSE LARVAE ARE EFFECTIVE PREDATORS. MANY GARDENERS USE THEM TO GET RID OF PESKY BUGS.

Aphidoletes are very good at finding aphid colonies. In one scientific study, aphidoletes were able to locate the one plant with an aphid colony out of 75 total plants.

One **APHIDOLETE LARVA** needs to eat only 7 aphids to complete its life cycle, but it may eat as many as 80.

APHIDOLETES HAVE BEEN RECORDED ATTACKING AND EATING OVER 60 SPECIES OF APHIDS.

THE LARVAE OF APHIDOLETES HAVE INCREDIBLY POWERFUL JAWS THAT THEY USE TO CRUSH INSECTS.

AHOY! PIRATES ON BOARD

ANTHOCORIDAE, ALSO KNOWN AS "MINUTE PIRATE BUGS," ARE PREDATORS THAT FEED ON SMALLER INSECTS AND INSECT EGGS. THEY ARE CALLED PIRATE BUGS BECAUSE OF THEIR AGGRESSIVE NATURE.

MINUTE PIRATE BUGS feed on all the life stages of thrips, aphids, mites, and other small arthropods. They are not picky eaters.

BOTH ADULT AND NYMPH MINUTE PIRATE BUGS USE THEIR PIERCING MOUTHPARTS TO SUCK THE JUICE FROM OTHER INSECTS.

MINUTE PIRATE BUGS HAVE ADAPTED TO BE SPEEDY HUNTERS THAT CAN RUN DOWN AND CATCH THEIR PREY.

Adult minute pirate bugs are very small (about half the size of a grain of rice), but don't let their small size fool you. Their bite is very irritating!

Minute pirate bugs have been classified as extremely aggressive hunters that can kill as many as 12 thrips every day, and they tend to kill more than they actually eat.

THE AMAZING ARACHNOCAMPA

PREY INSECTS ARE OFTEN SCARCE IN CAVE ENVIRONMENTS, BUT THE STOMACHS OF *ARACHNOCAMPA* LARVAE HAVE EVOLVED TO BE ABLE TO GO WEEKS OR MONTHS WITHOUT FOOD.

ARACHNOCAMPA is a New Zealand gnat. As larvae they are formidable hunters, but as adults they spend their lives seeking out a mate and never eat.

AFTER CATCHING AND EATING ITS PREY, ARACHNOCAMPA LARVAE WILL RECYCLE AND REUSE THE STICKY THREAD SO THEY DON'T HAVE TO WASTE ENERGY BUILDING A NEW ONE.

Arachnocampa means "SPIDER WORM." Arachnocampa larvae live in caves, far from light or wind. They hang lines of sticky thread from the ceiling of the cave and illuminate their bodies to attract insects to the sticky traps.

165

PRAYING MANTIS, INSECT WARRIOR

Praying mantises are the only insects that can see in 3D! This ability helps them hunt prey.

PRAYING MANTISES HAVE SPIKES ON THEIR LEGS TO PIN THEIR PREY IN PLACE.

AN AFRICAN MANTIS TWISTS ITS ENTIRE LOWER BODY WHILE TURNING ITS HEAD AND THORAX TOWARD A PREDATOR TO APPEAR TALLER AND MORE FRIGHTENING.

MANTIDS are fierce hunters. They strike hard and fast and will even eat their own offspring or other mantids.

BATS OFTEN EAT PRAYING MANTISES, BUT THE BUGS HAVE EVOLVED THE ABILITY TO DETECT BATS' ECHO-LOCATION SOUNDS. WHEN APPROACHED BY A BAT, A PRAYING MANTIS DUCKS AND MOVES AWAY.

When they hatch, baby mantids raise their arms in the air (like a kung-fu move) to appear bigger to predators such as jumping spiders.

AMBUSH BUGS

AMBUSH BUGS SIT MOTIONLESS INSIDE A FLOWER AND WAIT FOR AN INSECT TO COME NEAR. THEY QUICKLY GRAB THE INSECT WITH THEIR LARGE, HOOKED FORELEGS AND INJECT IT WITH VENOM.

Ambush bugs have wings but rarely use them. They spend most of their time creeping around on plants.

AMBUSH BUGS COME IN A VARIETY OF COLORS LIKE GOLD, YELLOW, LEAF GREEN, TAN, BROWN, OR WHITE, OFTEN WITH DARK PATCHES OR BANDS. THESE COLORS HELP THEM BLEND IN WITH THEIR ENVIRONMENT ALMOST PERFECTLY!

Scientists aren't sure if ambush bugs are able to change colors like CHAMELEONS or if they simply find flowers and leaves that match their coloration and patterns.

Chapter 6
BRILLIANT BUGS

WITHOUT **INSECTS**, OUR LIVES WOULD BE LIMITED IN A NUMBER OF WAYS. MOST PEOPLE KNOW THAT INSECTS ARE IMPORTANT POLLINATORS FOR FLOWERS, BUT INSECTS ARE ALSO ESSENTIAL TO PRODUCING CROPS SUCH AS APPLES, BLUEBERRIES, CHERRIES, ORANGES, AND SQUASH. THEY ARE, INDEED, BRILLIANT BUGS.

SIZE SURPRISE

The giant **GIPPSLAND EARTHWORM** is the longest earthworm in the world. It can grow up to 6½ feet long (2 m). That's taller than the average human adult!

QUEEN ALEXANDRA'S BIRDWING
IS THE BIGGEST BUTTERFLY IN THE WORLD, WITH A WINGSPAN OF 11 INCHES (28 CM). THAT'S ABOUT AS WIDE AS A TOASTER OVEN!

After feeding, **TICKS** can grow from the size of a grain of rice to the size of a marble.

The world's biggest snail is the **GIANT AFRICAN LAND SNAIL**, which is about the size of an adult human's hand.

THE GOLIATH BIRDEATER IS A HUGE TARANTULA THAT CAN EAT ENTIRE BIRDS OR MICE.

173

GLOW UP

GLOWWORMS
PRODUCE LIGHT TO WARN PREDATORS THAT THEY TASTE NASTY.

An **OSTRACOD** is a unique crustacean that shoots light out of its body and into the water. This helps it find mates and avoid predators.

BIOLUMINESCENCE OCCURS WHEN LIVING THINGS PRODUCE LIGHT THROUGH CHEMICAL REACTIONS IN THEIR BODIES.

SCORPIONS HAVE A FLUORESCENT MINERAL IN THEIR SKIN THAT MAKES THEM GLOW WHEN LIT UP WITH A BLACK LIGHT.

FIREFLIES ARE NOT THE ONLY ARTHROPODS THAT PRODUCE LIGHT. GLOWING GNATS AND SPRINGTAILS ALSO LIGHT UP THE NIGHT!

IT WOULD TAKE 70,000 FIREFLIES TO PRODUCE AS MUCH LIGHT AS ONE LIGHT BULB.

HUNGRY BUGS

THE **WEBBING CLOTHES MOTH** LOVES EATING THE CLOTHES IN YOUR CLOSET. IN THE WILD THEY FEED ON ANIMAL FUR.

SILVERFISH love books, but rather than reading them, they love eating the glue that binds the pages together.

A LADYBIRD BEETLE MAY EAT 5,000 INSECTS IN ITS LIFETIME! LADYBIRD BEETLES LIVE FOR A YEAR, SO THAT'S ABOUT 14 INSECTS A DAY.

SOME PLANTS RELEASE CHEMICALS THAT TRICK CATERPILLARS. WHEN THE CATERPILLARS SMELL THE CHEMICALS, THEY START EATING EACH OTHER INSTEAD OF THE PLANTS!

The larvae of *EPOMIS BEETLES* perform a dance that attracts frogs and toads. When a hungry frog or toad gets close, the larva attaches to the amphibian. The larva will then suck the frog or toad dry!

The larvae of the **GREATER WAX MOTH** can eat polyethylene, which is what plastic grocery bags are made of. Scientists are hoping that these larvae can get rid of plastic trash.

BUGS BUILT DIFFERENT

THE BRAZILIAN TREEHOPPER HAS HELICOPTER-LIKE APPENDAGES THAT STICK OUT FROM ITS HEAD. RESEARCHERS AREN'T SURE WHAT THEIR PURPOSE IS.

A CATERPILLAR HAS MORE MUSCLES THAN A HUMAN! A HUMAN HAS 650 TO 840 MUSCLES, AND A CATERPILLAR HAS AROUND 4,000, WITH 248 MUSCLES LOCATED JUST IN THE HEAD.

A YOUNG SNAIL PRODUCES A LIQUID THAT HARDENS INTO A SHELL OVER TIME. AS THE SHELL GROWS, IT COILS AROUND THE GROWING BODY OF THE SNAIL.

Have you ever wondered how flies hang upside down from the ceiling? Each of their feet has two claws. Under their claws are two sticky pads that grip the surface they're on.

THE BRAHMIN MOTH CATERPILLAR LOOKS LIKE SOMETHING FROM ANOTHER PLANET. IT HAS TENTACLE-LIKE SPINDLES GROWING FROM ITS ABDOMEN THAT DEFEND IT FROM PREDATORS.

EARTHWORMS have tiny bristlelike hairs on their bodies. When a bird tries to pull an earthworm out of the dirt, the earthworm uses its bristles to hold on to the soil!

INSECTS AT WORK

ABOUT ONE-THIRD OF ALL INSECT SPECIES ARE CARNIVOROUS AND PREFER TO HUNT OTHER INSECTS FOR THEIR MEALS.

ABOUT 2,000 SILKWORM COCOONS ARE NEEDED TO MAKE A SINGLE POUND OF SILK.

A POTTER WASP lays her eggs in tiny "POTS" made from mud and her own spit. She lays one egg into each pot with a paralyzed caterpillar for food, then seals the pot.

BLOWFLIES are the first insects on the scene when an animal has died. They are attracted to the smell of a fresh kill.

HONEYBEES need to make at least 10 million trips to collect enough nectar for one pound of honey!

ENGINEERING MARVELS

COLOBOPSIS EXPLODENS IS A SPECIES OF ANT THAT SELF-DESTRUCTS TO PROTECT THE COLONY. WHEN THE ANT SELF-DESTRUCTS, IT COVERS THE ENEMY IN A YELLOW GOO THAT EITHER KILLS THEM OR SLOWS THEIR ATTACK.

WATER SCORPIONS can breathe underwater with a snorkel-like tube that grows from their abdomen.

TO ENSURE THEY ALWAYS HAVE ENOUGH FOOD, HONEYPOT ANTS STORE FOOD IN THE BODIES OF CERTAIN ANTS CALLED REPLETES. THE REPLETES HANG UPSIDE DOWN FROM THE CEILING OF THE NEST UNTIL THE FOOD THEY CARRY IS NEEDED.

INDIAN MOON MOTHS CAN SMELL THE PHEROMONES OF A POTENTIAL MATE FROM MORE THAN 6 MILES (10 KM) AWAY!

HOUSEFLIES use sensors on their feet to find sugar. These sensors are 10 million times more sensitive than the human tongue.

A STICK BUG CAN GROW NEW LIMBS IF OLD LIMBS BREAK OFF.

TRAVELING BUGS

IN ORDER TO TRAVEL, A BEE'S WINGS NEED TO FLAP 190 TIMES PER SECOND, OR 11,400 TIMES PER MINUTE.

HUMANS HAVE SENT FRUIT FLIES INTO OUTER SPACE.

ANTS ARE SMALL, BUT THEY ARE INCREDIBLY FAST. AN ANT CAN TRAVEL AT A RATE OF ABOUT NINE BODY LENGTHS PER SECOND, WHICH IS EQUAL TO A HUMAN RUNNING 30 MILES (48 KM) PER HOUR.

It would take two hours for a common ground snail to cross the length of a football field.

A GRASSHOPPER, when jumping and flying, can reach speeds of up to 8 miles (13 km) per hour!

AWESOME ATHLETES

LEAFCUTTER ANTS CAN CARRY 50 TIMES THEIR BODY WEIGHT WITH JUST THEIR JAWS! THAT WOULD BE LIKE A HUMAN LIFTING A HIPPOPOTAMUS WITH THEIR TEETH.

The **HORNED DUNG BEETLE** can roll a dung ball that is 1,141 times its own body weight. That's like a single human pulling eight dump trucks!

The **GOLDEN WHEEL SPIDER** is an expert gymnast. When threatened, it pulls in its legs, throws itself to the side, and rolls in a tight ball. It's the only cartwheeling spider!

SOME MALE STONE FLIES DO PUSH-UPS TO ATTRACT A MATE.

JUMPING SPIDERS HOLD THE TITLE FOR THE BEST LONG JUMP. THEY CAN JUMP MORE THAN 40 TIMES THEIR BODY LENGTH. THEY ATTACH A SILK THREAD TO THEIR BODY THAT SERVES AS A BUNGEE CORD IN CASE THEY FALL.

The **CAT FLEA** is the champion of high jumps within the insect world. It can jump up to 150 times its own height. That's like a human jumping to the top of a 55-story building in one leap!

ARTHROPODS AT WORK

EARTHWORMS HELP KEEP THE SOIL HEALTHY. THEY EAT DECAYED LEAVES, DIGEST THEM, AND PRODUCE GOOD SOIL WHEN THEY POOP.

SCIENTISTS CAN USE BEE VENOM TO TREAT JOINT PAIN AND OSTEOPOROSIS IN HUMANS.

In some cultures, ANTS are used to close wounds like stitches. The ant latches onto the wound and closes its mouth, simultaneously closing the wound.

188

BUGS are natural recyclers! Insects eat fallen leaves and other plant debris and break them down into nutrients for plants.

HORSESHOE CRAB BLOOD IS A KEY INGREDIENT USED TO TEST NEW MEDICINES AND VACCINES.

HUMANS USE THE WEBS OF SPIDERS TO MAKE FISHING NETS, SURGICAL SUTURES, AND ADHESIVE BANDAGES.

COLORFUL CREATURES

AN **ORCHID MANTIS** HAS A COLORFULBODY AND LOOKS LIKE AN ORCHID FLOWER. ITS BEAUTIFUL COLOR AND FLOWERY DISGUISE ATTRACT INSECTS INTO ITS OPEN JAWS.

TWIG SPIDERS ARE NATIVE TO JAPAN, KOREA, AND CHINA, AND THEY AVOID GETTING EATEN BY PRETENDING TO BE TWIGS. THEY HAVE LONG, SLENDER BODIES WITH THIN LEGS TO MATCH.

TREEHOPPER NYMPHS HAVE THE WACKIEST HAIRDO IN THE INSECT WORLD. THEIR "HAIR" IS A WAXY SUBSTANCE THAT SCARES PREDATORS AWAY.

JUST LIKE THE BIRD IT IS NAMED AFTER, THE PEACOCK SPIDER HAS BEAUTIFUL COLORATIONS AND PATTERNS ACROSS ITS BODY THAT HELP ATTRACT MATES.

The PANDA ANT is the same color as a panda, but it isn't a panda or an ant. It is actually a wasp!

THE ARCHDUKE LARVA IS ONE OF THE MOST UNIQUE LOOKING LARVAE IN THE INSECT WORLD. ITS BODY IS COVERED IN BRANCHED SPINES WITH BLACK AND ORANGE TIPS THAT MAKE THE CATERPILLAR APPEAR UNFRIENDLY AND DANGEROUS.

191

BUGGING OUT!

THE VOODOO WASP LAYS NEARLY 80 EGGS INSIDE ONE CATERPILLAR. WHEN THE LARVAE HATCH, THEY BEGIN EATING THE CATERPILLAR FROM THE INSIDE OUT!

COCKROACHES can live for up to a week without their heads because they breathe through spiracles along their bodies instead of their mouths.

If more than one queen bee lives in a hive, the queen bees make a sound called **PIPING** to let the colony know that they will fight until there is only one queen. Their piping sounds like quacking!

The black-and-yellow **ASIAN SWALLOWTAIL** butterfly larva camouflages itself as bird poop to avoid being eaten.

SOME SPECIES OF LADYBUGS SQUIRT STINKY LIQUID FROM THEIR KNEES TO DETER PREDATORS ATTEMPTING TO EAT THEM.

MIDGE LARVAE can survive for up to three days in liquid nitrogen. Liquid nitrogen is about –321°F (–196°C). This is almost as cold as outer space!

193

THAT BUG DOES WHAT?

AMAZON ANTS STEAL THE LARVAE OF OTHER ANTS AND PUT THEM TO WORK IN THEIR COLONY. SOMETIMES THE ANTS THEY STEAL FIGHT BACK.

IN 2002, "CRAZY ANTS" WERE DISCOVERED IN TEXAS. WHAT MAKES THEM UNUSUAL IS THEIR ATTRACTION TO ELECTRICAL CORDS. THEY WILL CHEW ON WIRES INSIDE YOUR TV UNTIL THE ELECTRICAL SURGE KILLS THEM!

The **FUNGUS** known as *Ophiocordyceps* attacks the brains of ants. The fungus takes over the ant's body, making the ant behave like a zombie.

CROWS, HUMANS, AND ANTS ARE THE ONLY ANIMALS THAT FIGHT BATTLES IN FORMATION.

Researchers have found that **TERMITES** eat their food twice as fast when heavy metal music is playing.

PINE PROCESSIONARY CATERPILLARS CAN DESTROY ALMOST A WHOLE PINE FOREST IN A SINGLE GENERATION. ONCE THEY HAVE CONSUMED THE PINE NEEDLES OF ONE TREE, THEY MARCH IN A STRAIGHT LINE TO THE NEXT TREE.

195

BRILLIANT BUG: THE GIANT WETA

THE GIANT WETA MAY LOOK LIKE A HUGE CRICKET, BUT IT CAN'T JUMP! SOME OF ITS COUSINS, LIKE THE TREE WETA, CAN JUMP, BUT THE GIANT WETA IS EARTHBOUND.

THE GIANT WETA IS CLOSE TO EXTINCTION. WHEN HUMANS ARRIVED IN NEW ZEALAND MANY HUNDREDS OF YEARS AGO, THEY INTRODUCED RATS TO THE ECOSYSTEM. SINCE THEN RATS HAVE EATEN ALMOST ALL OF THE GIANT WETAS.

THE GIANT WETA IS ONE OF THE LARGEST INSECTS IN THE WORLD. IT CAN WEIGH MORE THAN A MOUSE!

THE GIANT WETA'S NAME MEANS "GOD OF UGLY THINGS."

THE GIANT WETA HAS EARS ON ITS KNEES.

When the giant weta is being preyed on, it uses its hind legs to make a loud hissing sound.

WAIT, THAT'S NOT AN ANT!

ANT-MIMICKING JUMPING SPIDERS NOT ONLY MIMIC ANTS IN APPEARANCE, THEY ALSO ACT LIKE ANTS. THEY CONSTANTLY WAVE THEIR FRONT LEGS AROUND LIKE ANTENNAE.

ANT-MIMICKING LONGICORN BEETLES resemble larger soldier ants. These beetles are harmless, so they pretend to be tough soldier ants for protection.

ANTS HAVE ALL KINDS OF DEFENSE MECHANISMS, LIKE PRODUCING AN ACIDIC TASTE, AGGRESSIVE BITING, AND PAINFUL STINGS. NO WONDER SO MANY INSECTS MIMIC THESE TINY WONDERS IN A PROCESS KNOWN AS MYRMECOMORPHY, OR ANT MIMICRY.

KATYDID NYMPHS mimic black ants in appearance to avoid predators while they are still young and vulnerable.

Ant-mimicking spiders pretend to be ants by using chemicals that allow them to attract and hunt down real ants.

Krystal Monique Toney is a PhD student at the University of North Texas, where her research focuses on the disparities in access to conservation education and nature among students in Texas. She founded the organization Black in Nature to share knowledge, creativity, and love for nature while simultaneously encouraging others to love and embrace the beauty of our natural world. Connect with her and her work at BlackinNature.com.

Printed in the USA
CPSIA information can be obtained
at www.ICGtesting.com
LVHW061531111223
765798LV00006B/2